Release t

Forgiving T

MW01716455

Written By Tonya Maxwell

MPowering Legacy Publishing

Published in the United States by MPowering Legacy Publishing, a sub-company of MPowering Legacy, LLC, Mississippi.
www.mpoweringlegacy.com

Tonya Maxwell
Release the Butterflies: Forgiving Those Who Hurt You

Version 1- October 3, 2023
ISBN: 979-8-9859450-7-2

Manufactured in the United States of America.
Printed in the United States of America

Dedication

This book is dedicated to all the courageous women who have faced abuse with unwavering strength, resilience, and courage - this book is a tribute to your remarkable spirit. Through your pain, you have found the power to heal; through your scars, you have discovered the beauty of your true self. May this book serve as a beacon of hope and empowerment for every woman who seeks to break free from the chains of abuse. No matter the circumstances, the human spirit can emerge stronger, more vibrant, and more alive.

You Can Live Triumphantly,

Coach Tonya

Contents

Introduction

Release the Butterflies - Forgiving Those Who Hurt You is a powerful initiative that aims to break down the barriers of fear, guilt, and shame that have silenced the voices of many. The initiative seeks to provide a platform for these voices to be acknowledged and empowered. We hope that by listening to these stories of forgiveness, you will be inspired to embark on a journey towards your own glorious future. The true gift of forgiveness is not only found in these stories, but it is revealed through the experience of it.

In the stories shared by Izzie, Ms. Kay, and Tonya you will witness the resilience of these women as they have dedicated their lives to supporting other survivors by raising awareness that this pervasive issue still exists worldwide, and that we all have a responsibility to confront this evil and to provide supportive resources to promote healing to those affected. These courageous women's journeys are also a testament that we all have the power within to rise above the trauma we may have experienced.

"Rise, take up your bed, and walk" were the words that Jesus spoke in those days, and the command still holds true today. (John 5:8)

3 In these lay a great multitude of sick people, blind, lame, paralyzed, waiting for the moving of the water.

4 For an angel went down at a particular time into the pool and stirred up the water; then whoever stepped in first, after the stirring of the water, was made well of whatever disease he had.

5 Now, a certain man was there who had an infirmity for thirty-eight years.

6 When Jesus saw him lying there and knew that he had already been in that condition a long time, He said, "Do you want to be made well?"

7 The sick man answered Him, "Sir, I have no man to put me into the pool when the water is stirred up, but while I am coming, another steps down before me."

8 Jesus said to him, "Rise, take up your bed, and walk."

9 And immediately the man was made well, took up his bed, and walked. - John 5:3-9 (NIV)

It was August 4th, 1998. As I was sitting in my living room, many revelations flooded my heart and mind. I thought of this broken man who is depicted in the parable. I could relate to those who required healing and empathized with their situation. I was sick. I was brokenhearted, paralyzed in pain. I felt a heavy cloud of unforgiveness that had deeply permeated my being. The place where I found myself was definitely not where I wanted to be. Similar to this man, I had been trapped in this state of brokenness for many years.

At one point, I didn't think I had the strength to take action for my own healing. I was hoping for someone else to come and rescue me, or at least that's what I wanted to believe. But if I'm being honest with myself, I had grown accustomed to being comfortable in the uncomfortable place of brokenness. It was all I knew, and I had resigned myself to the fact that life was always going to be this way for me. I would have to answer that same call just as this man did.

"Do you want to be made well?"

"I want to be well, Lord."

"Then, rise, take up your bed, and walk."

After struggling with affliction, self-pity, negativity, low self-esteem, and self-sabotage, God instructed me to rise above it all and become a witness for Him. His purpose was to use my life as a testimony of His love, mercy, and the fact that healing is possible. No matter what kind of trauma we may experience, triumph is always on the other side. Revelation 12:11 tells us that we can overcome the evil forces that come to accuse us, hinder our growth, and certainly want to make us doubt God's existence through two essential elements: Jesus' blood and our own testimonies. Let it be clear, we all have a part to play in our own healing. I was on my journey of healing and restoration. God was not only going to restore me; He was going to make me *Beaupaintiful (the state of being full of beauty despite the pain that one experiences).*

"Tonya," God called my name. "Get up, now it is your turn."

Just as Jesus spoke to the man at the pool, He also spoke to me. Just as He called my name and told me to get up and live, for it is my time, He is calling you too. Arise, my friend, this is your time to embrace your journey to heal, write your new chapter, and wear your crown. I hope that you will be encouraged as you read the compelling journeys of Izzy, Ms. Kay, and myself who found our healing and restoration from the brokenness of sexual abuse through our faith and the miraculous gift of forgiveness. This book is a witness to all those who desire to be well.

We encourage you to work alongside a spiritual counselor, your pastor or community place of worship leaders, a certified mental health therapist or other transformational support specialist to help you process the emotions that you may experience and assist you with developing strategies for transformation and personal growth. We send our sincere prayers to Heaven for you. We are so sorry that you are hurting because of what happened to you. We want you to know that you are not what happened to you. You are worthy of your healing. We, here at Triumphators, are standing with you. We celebrate you. Let's take a step forward together and boldly support each other by openly sharing our struggles, working through them, and empowering one another. Let your healing journey begin.

Coach Tonya

Tonya's Journey

The Residue of Sexual Abuse

Sexual abuse is unfortunately a topic that is often shrouded in stigmas and taboos. However, openly discussing it can greatly assist survivors in accessing the resources and support services they need to begin the healing process. The impacts of sexual abuse can be significant and prolonged, resulting in feelings of shame, guilt, and fear that may persist for many years. It is not uncommon for survivors to continue to face challenges such as trust issues, difficulty forming healthy relationships, and intimacy problems, even after the abuse has ended. It is crucial that we work to break the silence and stigma surrounding sexual abuse to provide survivors with the help and support they need to move forward.

It is crucial to acknowledge the long-lasting impact of sexual abuse on survivors, who often struggle with its residue. It is vital to extend support and empathy to those who have been affected by it. Sharing their experiences can help survivors connect with these resources and get the assistance they need There are several organizations, therapists, and support groups that specialize in helping survivors to express their emotions, process their trauma, and begin the journey of recovery. By speaking about their experiences, survivors may find validation for their pain and gain a sense of empowerment. By openly speaking about our personal experiences with sexual abuse, we aim to raise awareness about its prevalence and the negative impact it has on the lives of its victims. Our goal is to use our stories to educate society, challenge harmful beliefs and attitudes, and promote changes in policies, laws, and cultural norms to prevent sexual abuse and support other survivors. Moreover, we hope that by sharing our personal experiences, we can inspire other survivors who may be struggling in silence. Remember, you are not alone, and there is hope for healing and recovery.

Seeking help means you have taken a courageous step towards healing and living a fulfilled life. We pray that our stories will be a source of strength and encouragement for others on their healing journeys.

When I think back and reflect on how the sexual abuse impacted my life, I just think about the betrayal and the level of pain that I experienced. I had become so attached to the pain of the sexual abuse; it had become a part of me . . . a big part of who I was. I associated my existence with the pain. I lived it. I remembered it. I hid it from others. I hid it from me. The effects of the sexual abuse were deeply woven into my mind, body, and spirit. It was what I knew it to be. I did not know if these acts of violence were right or if they were wrong. I only knew how it (the abuse) made me feel.

I can remember the day as if it was yesterday. I was about nine years old when I came to understand that what had been happening to me had a name. I stumbled upon a book at a family member's house. I don't recall the title of the book, but the story that I read I can never forget. The person was telling a story of what was happening to her. She talked about the touching, the kissing, and everything that this person was doing to her when she was a little girl and how she felt *bad, sad, dirty, ashamed*, and *confused*. It sounded like what was happening to me: ***MO/LES/TA/TION.*** I was gasping for my breath. I was frozen in time. Oh, what does this mean? Am I in trouble now?

After reading that book, I would quietly return it to its original spot. However, for the following years, MOLESTATION, my enemy, would continue to haunt me. My mind was constantly plagued by the memory of that first event and every subsequent event that followed, along with the feeling of betrayal that came with it. It was an overwhelming and confusing mix of emotions. I couldn't understand how those who were supposed to love and protect me could be capable of causing me such harm. The same question kept resurfacing: *What happened? Was it right or wrong?*

That innocent four-year-old little girl was abducted. That friend of the family . . . they called him Reverend . . . he was the initiator of her abduction when he made the horrible decision to touch (her) me. Then, it was like he left an *open sign* on me, and the floodgates of this enemy,

MOLESTATION, had his way with me over the course of twelve long years. There were so many different faces and places of events, but that same enemy showed up every time. He showed up so much that I got used to him. Every time, I just wanted *it* to be over. That is how I got through each event. I knew that it would soon be over. I don't even remember crying. I was not afraid of *him* anymore. It was like his existence was stored in my body, and my soul was lost in outer space.

Survivors of sexual abuse may experience emotional numbness as a protective mechanism to cope with the overwhelming pain and distress. Alternatively, some may experience intense and fluctuating emotions, including anger, fear, sadness, and shame. During this time, I was so detached from myself that I could not process the pain, the betrayal, or the hatred. I know that it was there because of what I started doing to myself and what I believed about myself.

I internalized that pain into self-destructive behaviors that led me to engage in risky sexual behavior in response to trauma. I became promiscuous in the quest of looking for love, protection, and validation. Due to the trauma of the sexual abuse, one might even ask, "You like boys?" Yes, I did! I was looking for love, not sex. My innocence was not only broken; it was stolen. My young mind was trained to believe that sex was love, and we know that is not true. You can have sex with NO LOVE and you can have love with NO SEX.

The impact of the sexual abuse made it difficult for me to set boundaries, and it affected my ability to establish healthy relationships, especially relationships with men. As I reflect on the many relationships that I have encountered, I realize that this lack of trust was towards people in general. I was always quietly searching for their ulterior motive behind what they really wanted from me. Father, mother, sister, brother, uncle, aunt, friends, or co-workers, what do they want from me?!

That little voice was so loud as it screamed within. Sometimes it felt as if blood-sucking leeches were all over me, pulling, poking, picking, and the wind kept winding. I did not know how to remove them, so I accepted that gruesome picture and its pain. I just did not have the energy to search out their intentions. The residue that this evil left behind caused me not to trust my own judgment or my own intentions. That sense of safety did not exist anymore. That had been shattered. I even took the risk of getting in cars with strangers and meeting up with them. Thank God I am still here today to share my story.

That self-abusive behavior that I spent most of my lifetime trapped in influenced some of the same destructive behaviors that many women have found themselves pattering. I, as well as many other survivors of sexual abuse, are at an increased risk of experiencing revictimization or further instances of abuse, as we may be vulnerable to abusive relationships or engage in risk-taking behaviors. From my teenage years until age forty, I experienced this horrific cycle of dead-end relationships. It was like I was drawn to those types of relationships because that was what I believed love relationships were about. It would take years and a lot of work for me to begin to understand what true intimacy was. I was co-dependent on the pain. No matter how disappointing those relationships were, I allowed myself to stay. It was about me denying my own happiness and self-fulfillment in order to perform to please others. I was not the priority.

Sexual abuse can have profound and long-lasting effects on the survivors. The impact can vary depending on factors such as the severity and duration of the abuse, the survivor's age at the time of the abuse, the presence of support systems, and the individual's coping mechanisms. Sexual abuse can lead to various psychological effects as well. I can identify with the women who have shared their stories about their battles with post-traumatic stress disorder (PTSD), anxiety, depression, and other mental health disorders, as well as feelings of low self-esteem, shame and guilt, self-blame, and dissociation. Many of us may experience recurrent nightmares and flashbacks that are triggered by scents, songs, places, and people, especially those in authority. Many women also report how they are battling with self-image distortion.

Some survivors may turn to substance abuse, while others suffer from eating disorders to cope with the emotional pain and distress caused by the abuse. I did not like the fact of being high (not being aware of what was happening around me), so drinking and drugs were not my go-to vice. I enjoyed eating food. It was during my healing journey that I learned the reason behind my secret affection for food. I would not have thought that I was displaying disordered eating behaviors, but I was. I used to hide food in my room in the dresser drawers, under my pillow, under the bed, or in my closet. At night, in my hiding place, I would soothe myself with food while everyone else was sleeping.

These actions were definitely related to those secrets. I was mishandled in secret, and I ate in secret. I was good at keeping secrets to the point I never told a soul for at least two years when I started having my monthly visitation, if you know what I mean. Why? Why didn't I tell my mother, or even my older sisters for that matter? As a young girl among friends, they would share their stories of coming into womanhood, but not me. So many things happen in life that we can't control. I guess I was exercising my right to control that part of my vagina. We were safe during this time of the month. It was just me, myself, and her (my period). No one else. I had something that no one could control or take from me. She was the boss during that time. Nobody wanted her anyway. My period took care of me, and I took care of her.

Little Tonya was like a superhero to me. I can remember how she protected me. I really depended on her a lot. She had a sense of what I call "boldnacity"- a state of firmly holding on to the spirit of courage no matter the circumstance one is experiencing. She was trying to protect me in every way possible that she knew existed. She took the blunt force of the abuse, even though she did not know how just to SAY NO. From the tender age of five or six, she would parade around the house, seeing who she could pick up. This included grown-ups too. She was flexing her muscles. She was trying to prove that no matter what people were doing to her, she was strong; however, she needed to be rescued too. I wanted to help her escape from the enemy who had set out to destroy her. I just didn't know how.

The pain of the sexual abuse was immensely unbearable. On October 4, 1988 at 18 years old while away at college, I attempted suicide. I wanted the pain to end. I was beyond desperate. I felt as if I was alone. I had no one that I could talk to that would understand what I had gone through, nor could they help me. During that time, I saw death as the only way out. My heart just wanted to stop hurting. My mind just wanted to be free from the agony. The dark agony was torturing me daily, and I was hoping that death would free me.

Individuals who either feel trapped in distressing situations or experience a prolonged sense of hopelessness may perceive suicide as a way to escape their pain. They may believe that their circumstances are unbearable and see no other viable options for relief or improvement as I did.

If you or someone you know is experiencing a mental health crisis, please know that you are not alone. Call the Suicide Prevention Hotline at 988 for immediate support.

Don't try to handle things on your own. It almost cost me my life. Sooner or later things will come crashing down. It is okay to not to be okay. Get help. You owe it to yourself. I thank God for my life today. While I was fighting to die, Terry, one of my college roommates, was fighting for me to live. I mean, literally, we were fighting. That fight led me to the toilet water. I will discuss that in full detail in my book titled Help, I'm Desperate: The Suicide Attempt that Saved Me. If I had passed away, I would have missed so many blessings that I have received despite the trauma. That means that I would have missed this opportunity to be here in this present moment, sharing my journey with you. You see, all that I have gone through really was not just about me. It is about you, too. I needed to be here, as my destiny would have it, to encourage you to know that you can make it. You are going to make it to the other side.

So where did I go from there? How did I move forward to the point where I am today? Well, my friend, I am glad that you asked. October 5th, 1988, I wrote I know in my heart that it was God that saved me. He sent Terry to the rescue. I was convinced that God wanted me to live. Why? I am not sure, but I am here for a reason. In my lack of understanding my purpose, why am I here? Why did God allow me to survive that suicide attempt? What I had experienced was dim, dark, and ugly. I did not want any parts of it. I wanted to forget the heartache and the pain. Since God allowed me to live, I believed that I needed to forget the past if I was going to be happy.

I would spend the next ten years fervently praying for amnesia. I was convinced that if I was going to live, surely God was going to answer my prayer. So, I kept on praying every single day. "Lord, give me amnesia. I don't want to remember what I have gone through." And lo and behold, God answered. I was watching a Christian Evangelist on television. He was praying for the people, and the words that I heard him say would forever, and I mean forever, change my life. He said, "There is a woman out there who has been praying for amnesia." I almost jumped into that TV.

"YESS, I'm gon' get it today!!!" I was ready. God had FINALLY heard my prayer. . . Wheeeew! So, I had my hands in the air surrendering to the call to receive what God had for me: my gift of amnesia.

The words that I would hear next were, "God wants you to know that you are NOT going to get amnesia. You will remember what you have gone through. God knows that He can trust you to speak of His goodness, mercy, and kindness regardless of your past. God is going to use your story for His Glory."

As you can imagine, I was like "WHAT!!! WAIT A MINUTE. God, you have been hearing my prayers all this time?" I was excited to know that He heard me but was confused about why it took Him so long to answer me. As I cried out in a state of relief on one hand and confusion on the other, I said, "Lord, if you are not going to give me amnesia, then remembering all that I have gone through has to be for Your glory." I truly did not understand what my life was going to be or how God was going to use me, but I felt as if He was calling me to a place of healing and restoration. Over the next several years, I traveled a path "in the valley of the shadows of death." I had to come to the terms that I had been sexually abused repeatedly and that I was not going to forget that it happened to me. God, in His infinite wisdom, purposed for me to remember what happened. God was leading me through that path of His righteousness as He prepared the journey for me to forgive those who had trespassed against me as He was cleansing my heart.

To be honest, my friend, that valley was a trying place for me. I was afraid. I wanted them to pay for what they did to me. I wanted them to be put on display and feel the shame, guilt, and humiliation that I was feeling. I didn't want to forgive them because I was angry about what they had done. Anger had found its way to my heart. I simply wanted them, all of them, to die so that they could not hurt anyone else. Ultimately, I thought their death would take my pain away too.

In closing, when overcoming sexual abuse through forgiveness, let us remember that forgiveness is not about forgetting. It's about reclaiming our lives, our identities, and our peace. It's about choosing love over hate, strength over weakness, and liberation over captivity. Forgiveness is a testament to our journey of how we traveled from Trauma to Triumph.

My Act of Forgiveness

Many people are resistant to forgiveness because they do not understand the value of forgiveness. I recall the moment when God told me that He was calling for me to be the bigger person to forgive those who hurt me. I will never forget that day. You can imagine the exclamation in my voice.

"What? Why? Who me? Why do I have to be the bigger person? I did not do them wrong; they hurt me. They abused me!" I screamed and cried uncontrollably, "Why ME? Why do I have to do this, Lord God? This is so unfair."

Well, all I can say is that I was not prepared for the response I received:

"Because I said so."

August 4th, 1998 was a day that forever changed my life. It was a pivotable turn that had to be taken and that journey began with me surrendering myself to the Lord. I was on a three-day fast with no food or water. I was desperate. I needed to hear from God. What was the plan that He had for me? During this fast, I decided to use all my energy to hear from Him. On day two He spoke.

"Tell your story; it shall be a testimony, your encouragement of praise. It is a banner of invitation to the Lord for those paths you are destined to cross. God told me that He anointed me to go through the *fire* because He knew that I would surrender to His voice, and while still in pain, I would praise Him. God knew that I would come out of hiding to be a witness to encourage other women who are broken-hearted because of the sexual abuse. There is a lot of brokenness in the nation, but God, in His divine plan of order, is bringing restoration to His people. His plan to use me for His glory had begun to be clear to me as I intentionally worked on myself and submitted my life to the Lord. This journey will take the rest of my life to complete. I had to say yes to the call first to be made well.

I say this with sensitivity and all due respect, the memory of what happened will be with you, and the key to your healing is not simply sweeping it under the rug, nor keeping it at the forefront of your mind reliving it as a victim. The key to healing is releasing the anger and resentment surrounding the event(s). Even for the deepest of wounds, it is crucial to find a healthy way to detach as much as possible from the pain, not the memory. In most cases, this means moving into a state of forgiveness for the one who caused the wound, as well as forgiving yourself. This was the place where God called me. Holding on to the pain was unproductive, and I kept living as a victim of my past. So, today I choose to forgive and move on from the agony of my past. It is not because I forgot about what happened. I stopped allowing the past to control me, my present, and my glorious future. Guess what? I forgive myself, too. I will continue to show self-compassion towards myself to get rid of the constant reminders of the mistakes that I have made.

God knew that my true healing was not in the place of simply getting amnesia or subconsciously not remembering what happened. It was in the place of releasing what had been woven so deeply within my being: the anger, hatred, resentment, and the negative image I had about myself. I had to stop running from what happened. God did not want me to be just like *anyone* else. Anyone can hold on to anger, but it takes a humble person, that person who wants to be well, to forgive those who hurt them. He knew that He made me special. He just needed me to experience it. I had to *Release The Butterflies and Forgive Those Who Hurt Me.* The beauty of my healing, your healing, is experiencing the freedom to fly from the cocoon and allowing the world to be in awe of the beautiful colors that encompass our journey. I was broken sitting on the side of the pool of despair. Jesus called me by my name.

"Tonya, do you want to be well?"

I said, "Yes."

I picked up my bed and walked. I count it great joy that God has put His trust in me, and in my obedience, many lives shall be changed.

Reflection:

1. Have you considered that some individuals may not forgive because they believe it lets the offender off the hook for their actions?

2. *What would you say to someone who argues that forgiveness can lead to repeated offenses and a lack of accountability for the offender?*

3. *How would you address those who believe that forgiveness requires an apology or acknowledgment of wrongdoing from the offender?*

Affirmation:

While I may have been wronged in the past, I choose to forgive others. Forgiveness is a gift I give myself. By forgiving others, I become free of the past. I am, then, free to live entirely in the present and look forward to my glorious future.

Live Life Triumphantly

Izzie's Journey

I was Hurting so I Hurt Others

Izzie shares her story of how the effects of sexual abuse impacted her life. Not only was she hurting, but she hurt other people. As we walk through the journey of her story, we will see how she entered her path of wholeness. Izzie has shared her journey here with us as well as on other platforms to inspire other women on how to gracefully move beyond the veil of shame and guilt of what happened to them.

A lot of times I allowed what others had done to me or what they said about me to control my actions, my thoughts, and my dreams. For a long time, at least as long as I can recall, I was in my thirties, and I believed that my body was *the best thing* I had to offer. No one had ever shown love and kindness towards my womanhood. I did not either. I was in and out of so many sexual relationships as a teenager, and unfortunately, it carried over into my adulthood.

Sex was introduced to me at a young age and beauty it never beheld. It became a tool that I learned to use to cover up the feelings of abandonment, fear, and loneliness as a result of the sexual abuse that I experienced. I would become my own sex abuser, and in that pain, I hurt other people. This is what I was taught. This is what I received. This is what I had done. Let me make it clear. I am not saying that I molested children. No, no, no. What I am saying is that I used sex, not in the beautiful way in which God purposed it, but I used it as a weapon.

I tried it all: sex before marriage, sex with my boyfriends, with their friends, sex with myself, and having five children before marriage. I thought about trying same-sex relationships. Maybe that would make me better. I even considered doing drugs. Oh, I even tried lying and cheating, and would you believe it, I tried abstinence, too. None of that worked for me or would ever work because at the root of all my intentions was hurt and despair that continued to spin out of control.

What I have come to understand while on my healing journey, individuals, including myself, who have experienced trauma or significant pain may often carry deep unresolved emotional wounds. When these wounds are left unaddressed or untreated, they can manifest as unresolved anger, resentment, or distress, which can be projected onto others, and this is exactly what I was doing. I was projecting my pain onto other people. I was in a vicious dysfunctional circle going around and around.

I tried to find completion, wholeness, and freedom through these young men, who without a doubt were not capable of doing so. From one lover to the next in desperation, I was on a search, and at times I did not take others' feelings into consideration. It was like love them (have sex) and leave them. The craziest thing about it was I was not leaving them. I was keeping them locked in the jail cell of my own misery. Talk about misery loves company.

I mishandled them, and I mishandled myself. I was projecting my own pain, anger, and insecurities onto them. By directing my own negative emotions outward, for a split second at times, I temporarily alleviated my own discomfort and shifted the focus away from my pain of guilt. I created reasons for why I could not continue to see them. I blamed them for our breakups; it was all their fault. I was so broken. It seems to me that somehow I took pleasure in seeing them cry when I said it was over. Their tears consoled me. "*Well, at least he loves me,*" I thought. Yet that was only a temporary high. I spent decades crying about what was done to me and what I had done to others.

Hurt individuals may struggle with empathizing with others or regulating their own emotions. Their pain and unresolved issues can make it difficult for them to understand or connect with the feelings and needs of others. Some individuals who have been victims of abuse themselves may repeat the cycle. They may mistakenly believe that hurting others will provide them with a sense of power or control, mirroring the dynamics they experienced in their own victimization. As a result, they may engage in hurtful behaviors without considering the impact on others.

I wanted to be in control because I had no control over those who decided to hurt me. I keep them locked away one after the other, hoping someday that one of them could just get it right. I was holding them captive because I was yearning for an apology from those whom I trusted who sexually abused me. I needed to hear them say that they were sorry for what they had done to me. I needed to hear my father say that he was sorry. I needed to hear my uncles say they were sorry. I needed to hear my cousin say he was sorry.

The sexual abuse distorted the true meaning of love for me. I felt as if I was not worthy of real love, unconditional love, or self-love. Their actions caused me not to trust even those who were trustworthy. I often wondered what happened to them. What traumatic experience(s) were they holding on to that caused them to hurt me?

When hurt individuals have not learned healthy ways to process their pain and emotions, they may resort to harmful behaviors as an attempt to cope. This can include lashing out, aggression, manipulation, or engaging in destructive patterns of behavior. This is why it is imperative that a survivor of sexual abuse work with a support team to help individuals access appropriate professional help, such as therapy or counseling, to aid them in processing the pain of the trauma in order to promote personal growth and positive change.

I wanted change, but I did not know where to begin. I had done so much, and I guess I really thought that having peace, joy, and happiness, well, was just in the movies. All of the relationships that I witnessed in my reality were all dysfunctional. Verbal abuse, divorce, fornicating, living out of wedlock, addiction, bad credit, revenge, lack of commitment, lying, cheating, laziness, promiscuity, perversion, depression, anxiety, and lots of stress and health issues, and unforgiveness were what I saw, what I believed, what I did, too. Even though we were in church daily from sun up to sun down, these issues were not addressed. Our family wore the mask. We witnessed all this madness, but no one talked about the elephant(s) in the room, not even the sexual abuse.

Any trauma specialist will agree that when families refuse to address or acknowledge the sexual abuse, the family may inadvertently perpetuate the harm experienced by the survivor. Denial and avoidance of the issue can prevent the survivor from receiving the support, validation, and healing they need. It may lead to feelings of isolation, self-blame, and shame for the survivor, hindering their recovery process. I believe that this is one of the main reasons there was so much drug and alcohol addiction in my family. I could be wrong, but I believe that this didn't just happen to me. There were just too many perpetrators. Things like this are spiritual, and they have the tendency to move from one generation to the next and on and on. I believe that this vicious thing just kept happening over and over, victim after victim, because no one talked about it. Growing up in the South, we were taught that you don't air your dirty laundry out for everyone to see. So, you just didn't tell. You just didn't tell.

To tell you the truth, it was not about you telling something that was unknown. Oh, I believe people knew what was going on. You just didn't TALK about what was going on. I can remember one summer, I had gone to visit my auntie and uncle, and I had fallen asleep on the sofa that night. I guess he waited until he thought my auntie was asleep. He slipped out of bed, picked me up from the sofa, took me into the guestroom, and proceeded to start his shenanigans, you know. Oh, but wouldn't you know who came looking for him . . . right.

Auntie was up on a hunt when she came busting into the room, and it was the sound of her voice that made me know she knew what he was doing. When you catch someone red-handed and you ask, "WHAT ARE YOU DOING?!", you know what they are doing. He answered like a kid who got caught with his hand in the cookie jar.

"I ain't doing nothing, just putting her to bed that's all."

The next morning, he came and whispered, "If your auntie asks you what I was doing last night, just tell her I was putting you to bed. Okay? I was just putting you to bed."

That scenario played in my head for years. I kept hearing her say that over and over again, "WHAT ARE YOU DOING?! WHAT ARE YOU DOING?! WHAT ARE YOU DOING?! "WHAT ARE YOU DOING?! WHAT ARE YOU DOING?!" The saddest thing is she never asked me. Then one day I heard my mother screaming and crying that her baby sister had died. I was always hoping that she would just ask me what he was doing that night. My auntie has been dead for many years, God rest her soul, and I can still hear her saying, "WHAT ARE YOU DOING?!" I'm not sure if I would have had the strength to tell her what he was doing, but I'm sure my tears would have.

I was angry with my auntie for a long time. I loved her, but I hated that she never asked me the question or even talked to me about not allowing anyone to touch me, you know. What I believe is that family members who are aware of the sexual abuse but choose not to talk about it, become screwed up too. Guilt, shame, denial, or conflicting emotions can arise from not addressing the issue, leading to negative impacts on their mental well-being. Maybe this is what killed her.

Out of all the times that my uncle abused me, this was the time that really hurt me the most because I now knew that all this while he talked about this being *our little secret*, but it was not a secret. It was the *family secret* everybody was aware of but nobody would confront. I stayed imprisoned in that moment for years. That prison cell is what haunted me. It was the reason behind all those whom I held there with me, my POWs. I could not free them because I was not free.

Sexual abuse within a family can strain relationships and disrupt family dynamics. When the issue is not addressed, it can create a sense of division, secrecy, and tension within the family. Family members may experience difficulties in relating to one another, leading to distance, conflict, or a breakdown in relationships. Not only that, but it can also create this strain in all other relationships. I think that we are taught to have such an allegiance within our family as we should, but not to the point where harm is being done, acts of violence are being committed, and we choose to stay silent.

Trauma has a way of stealing your voice, I know. I stayed silent for decades. Now, I go around the country sharing my story. I have talked to thousands of women and girls, but my family, no, not my family. I invite them, but they just don't show up. I get it. That's where many of them are, and I am okay with that. Hey, maybe they will listen to my podcasts and all. I just hope that they get the help that they need and deserve. It is critical that family members talk about this evil or the cycle will just continue. **It will never stop if it is allowed to remain in the dark.**

Sharing our stories as survivors of sexual abuse is a crucial step in breaking the cycle of darkness. By healing ourselves and finding forgiveness for those who have hurt us, we can become a beacon of hope for others who are still struggling. Our stories and resilience have the power to inspire, educate, and provide support to those who need it most. As I continue my own healing journey, I am committed to empowering the next generation of women and girls to find their own strength and resilience.

My Act of Forgiveness

As I said, I grew up in the church. We were there day and night. One Sunday the guest preacher was teaching on forgiveness. It was a four-day revival. The Bible has a lot to say about forgiveness, you know. Every day he would close out with a prayer, and then he would say, "Forgiving is not about the other person; forgiveness is for you." I asked him on the last day what he meant by that, and he explained that when someone wrongs you, forgiving them frees your heart from malice, bitterness, and hatred that you may have for that person. Then, he reminded me of the sermon he preached about how Jesus forgave those who crucified him. His act of forgiveness cleared the way for him to make it back to the Father in heaven.

---

*"Then Jesus said, '**Father, forgive them**; for **they** do not know what **they** are doing.' And **they** cast lots to divide his clothing."*

(Luke 23:34).

I studied those scriptures, especially Luke 23:34, and I prayed because I was struggling with the pain that I was experiencing from the sexual abuse. It just looked like everybody had gone on with their lives as if nothing had happened. They looked like they were having a jolly good ole time every day as if they had not wronged me. Meanwhile, I was struggling. I was angry to the point I started contemplating how I could hurt them and even get away with killing them for what they had done to me. I was in a very dark place at that time. I wanted to get them back.

When someone feels wronged, they may believe that seeking revenge is a way to help them feel better, establish their own voice, take the stand to say NO MORE, and ensure that the other person faces consequences for their actions, but my revenge was not God's plan.

Then it happened. I got a call from my uncle. As I answered the phone, I could hear someone sobbing on the line.

"I'm sorry!!! I'm sorry!!! I'm sorry!!!"

I was confused about what was going on. Initially, I thought it was someone playing a prank on the line. I did not even recognize his voice.

I kept saying, "Who is this? What do you want?"

Then that scripture flashed in my head and my heart like a lightning bolt. The tears just began to pour, not just from my eyes, but from my heart. The water of the word began to wash me at that moment.

My uncle would go on to say that he was sorry for what he had done to me and that he was sick and needed help because he had been abused, too. I had an overwhelming flood of emotions that I can't even describe, but those words the preacher said, *Forgiveness is not about the other person; forgiveness is for you* rang in my head. My uncle admitted that he was not making excuses for his actions. He was taking full responsibility for what he had done. At that moment, I was full of all kinds of emotions; I thought that I would immediately *feel better* hearing *I'm sorry*, but it did not happen just like that.

Even though he said he was sorry, the pain didn't just go away. What it did do was validate the hurt and the betrayal that I carried. It was not just in my head. I truly had a broken heart. It was up to me to release the pain. My healing was up to me. God would lead me back to the same words of forgiveness that Jesus spoke. Over the next twenty years, I worked on releasing the pain and the POWs that I held in the prison cell of my misery.

I stopped feeling sorry for myself, and not because what happened to me still does not make me feel sad. It does. I stopped living as a victim. I made it through by the grace of God. I was on the other side now, and I had the desire to tell my story. I want to be to other women and girls what I needed. I have created a safe space where people can come and share their stories. It is my life's work to encourage women to heal and move beyond their loss and their pain. As I continue to share, I am still healing. This journey is forever. I still cry at times, but these tears are tears of gratitude and humility. I cry with those who share. They need to know that it is okay to cry. Tears can evoke empathy and compassion in others. When people witness someone else crying, it often elicits a desire to offer comfort and support, fostering connection and empathy between individuals. Crying helps to release the pain. Crying clears the atmosphere for our healing. There is a lot to be said and to be shared but remember to take time to cry.

I was now able to open the prison doors and free my Prisoners of War: Kevin, Lenoard, Frank, "The Sand Man" James, Robert, Steve, Carl, Kenny, Victor, Joey, Kevin, Reggie, Craig, Lionel, Curtis, Ken, Derrick, Michael, Sean, Anthony, Paul, Danny, Roosevelt, Robbie, Kenny, Kevin, Terrell, Chuck, Ray, Alphonso, Michael, CJ, Mario, Winston, Josiah, and Lloyd. I want to say I am sorry. I apologize. Please, forgive me. I mishandled you. I kept you locked behind the walls of my pain and frustration, hoping one day that one of you could just get it right (make the pain disappear). I did not know that what I needed, you were not capable of giving me. The love that I needed I have found in Jesus, and through his gift of forgiveness and His loving-kindness, the void that the sexual abuse I experienced has been filled. You have served your time, the gates are open, and you are free to be free. Love the Lord, your wives, your children, and please love yourself. Go in peace, my brothers.

To those who were supposed to love and protect me, I had to really work at forgiving you for what you had done. I had to work through the flashbacks; oh boy, those years were very trying. If I heard your voices or saw you at family functions, I was fighting against those flashbacks. As the Lord continued to soothe my heart, those flashbacks began to vanish. I had to learn that I have the power to control my thoughts. I did not have to allow the bitterness to control me anymore. Even if what you did to me gave me the right to hate you, that same hate did not give me the right to be free. I choose to be free.

Jesus prayed for those who had betrayed, hated, and crucified Him without just cause. He said, "Father, forgive them, for they do not know what they are doing." -Luke 23:34 (NIV)

Reflection:

Forgiveness puts me back in control of my life. I focus on my own reactions rather than external events. My resilience increases as I become more skillful at dealing with conflicts and disappointments.

Ms. Kay's Journey

The Lost Jewel

When a person loses something valuable, it can lead to a sense of loss similar to experiencing bereavement. People may go through a grieving process, experiencing denial, anger, bargaining, sadness, and acceptance as they come to terms with the loss. Losing something valuable that holds sentimental or emotional significance can be particularly challenging, reminding the individual of cherished memories, special relationships, or experiences. Such a loss can intensify the emotional impact that a person may go through.

A person may feel regret or blame themselves for not being more careful or responsible, especially if they perceive their own actions or negligence as contributing to the loss. This adds to the emotional burden and makes it harder for the person to cope with the loss. Ms. Kay shares her journey about her lost jewel and how she overcame guilt, shame, hopelessness, and despair while on her journey to recovery.

During my childhood, I was abused by my pastor. I was nine years old when the abuse started. It would take me almost thirty years to find my way back to me: my happy place. These wounds ran deep. My childhood, my innocence, and the freedom to be me were stolen. My freedom to trust was shattered. All of me, mind, body, and spirit, had been abducted. The pastor was well-liked and an important role model in our community. Everybody just loved him and his family, and this is what made this experience even more traumatic. Our beloved pastor lit up the church with his hand clapping, foot stomping, and his voice that made every pitch on point as he escalated in his cadence when saying, “Can I get an Amen?” Now, that’s what my momma used to call having church. Who would ever believe that our pastor could be capable of harming children? I was a child back then so after the songs were over, I was just there because I did not have a foundation to understand the preached word at that time. So, we children either played between the pews (hoping not to get caught) or we nodded our heads and fought to keep our eyes open.

After Sunday service, we always had dinner at the church. It was like one big happy family. I can still remember the fried chicken those mothers of the church would make. That was everyone’s favorite as well as the peach cobbler, the apple pie, and the blueberry pie. I really loved going to church, and not just for the good food. Our Sunday School teacher would tell us these wonderful stories about Jesus and how He came to save us and protect us and that He was with us all the time. So, I was not afraid of anything. It was one Sunday afternoon when the pastor’s wife had been in the hospital and was due to come home, so I volunteered to go and help tidy things up around the house. Everything seemed okay, but there was something about the way that the pastor thanked me that day. As I reflect on things, something was just not right. His normal greetings of "Hello, Katie" and "How are doing today?" began to be weird. He would greet me with my family around as usual, then he would greet me again, alone. So, I did not know that there was something he had brewing, but there was. I simply thought that he was just happy that I was able to come and help the First Lady around the house. I suffered some disillusionment when I realized that what was involved was not right. It was not pure. It was not love. It was not Christian-like.

Hugging and greeting with an occasional kiss on the forehead were acceptable in my family as well as at church. Over the next three years, I spent a lot of time with Pastor and First Lady. Their home became like my second home. First Lady had gotten a lot better, and she was giving me piano lessons. I really grew very close to them. I really loved them, but the tables would soon turn. That happy place grew cold and sad, and I did not know why. Why was Pastor doing these strange things to me?

There was something very dark brewing behind those hugs and kisses. He began fondling me, caressing me, and kissing me. I was a victim of sexual abuse at nine years old. My parents were clueless. They had no idea of the things that he was doing to me, and to make matters worse, he would always say how special I was to him and his wife. He would say that I was a blessing to them. I was their answered prayer. God blessed them with a special helper—they wanted a daughter but did not have children of their own. People just did not know what his special really meant, not even the First Lady. The community really looked up to him; we all trusted him, and he misused his position.

To the outside world, I was the apple (the forbidden fruit) of his eye. I did not really understand that his hugs, kisses, and the LUST for me that he called love were not pleasing to God. I accepted it as this was okay. This was the way that it was supposed to be. After all, he was the pastor. His actions distorted my spiritual foundation and understanding of the type of love that God had prepared for me. His actions caused me to stumble and fall. I would soon question if I was important to God.

Misusing power often involves exploiting or taking advantage of others for personal gain or for self-gratification. This can manifest in various forms, such as financial exploitation, manipulation, discrimination, coercion, or abuse of authority, and it can definitely have serious consequences that can impact the lives of those affected for many years. It can cause physical, emotional, spiritual, and psychological harm that often leads to toxic work, social, or self spaces. I am not sure if there are other victims or if he exploited the church for financial gain, or any other privileges that he had received, but what I do know is that what he did to me changed me.

By the time I was thirteen years old, he was having an affair with me. I became the other woman. He treated me to the movies, dinner, shopping, and all sorts of fun things. He would even sneak me into his office and have his way with me. The entrapment of sexual sin and perversion was at the center of my core. The sexual abuse created a GIANT. That giant of sex addiction had begun to manifest. The first thought of the day was sex. The last thought of the day was sex. Rather, I was at school, home, or church at some part of the day, I was thinking about sex.

The sexual abuse made me believe that having sex was the answer to everything. If you want something, need something, or if you're sad or mad about anything, well you could fix it. Just have sex. It would fix all of your problems. Consequently, having sex was the problem. This appetite was growing in depth. I was having sex with him (the pastor), them (the church boys), and myself. Pornography was also introduced to me and that took on a course of destruction on its own. Of course, I did all these things in hiding. I was the good church girl on the outside.

My world came crashing down. At sixteen years old, I had gotten pregnant. I was not only in shock, but I was also afraid. This dilemma set in a storm of emotions. I was confused and sad, and a mix of different feelings overshadowed me. This was overwhelming as I was now faced with trying to process the news and consider my options. I had only one option. This is the option he, the pastor, gave me, and that was to get rid of it. As he explained, "We can't let anything spoil our special place, and having a baby now would spoil that. It would make the First Lady feel, you know, as if God had let her down." She could not have children.

As a teenage girl now faced with choices regarding this unplanned pregnancy, what was I to do? I thought about having the baby, and giving it up for adoption, or should I just have an abortion? I really did not want to have an abortion. I was against it. I believed that everyone deserved the chance to live, and here I was thinking about having an abortion. Now having to make such decisions was challenging, and I was emotionally full of despair. How was I going to explain to my parents, the church members, and the poor First Lady? The fear of being judged, shamed, or ostracized by friends, family members, and everyone else was just too much. I did not just feel bad about the pregnancy. The guilt and shame of what I had been doing, this sex thing, and this addiction sent me into an awful downward spiral.

Supportive and understanding family members, friends, or partners can provide emotional support, guidance, and assistance in decision-making. Conversely, a lack of support or negative reactions can exacerbate feelings of isolation, shame, or anxiety. Who could I turn to? Pastor already said what he wanted. That kept ringing in my head. Keep yourself for marriage was ringing in my head. All the things I had done were ringing in my head. I had nowhere to turn. It took me almost four months to make the decision to go through with the procedure. I was going to abort my innocent, unborn baby.

I showed up at the clinic on the very last day that they had given me to come in for the appointment. If I had not shown up, then it would be past the time that they could perform the procedure. The abortion clinic listened to me without judgment. Well, let me rephrase that. They did not listen to me; they did not approach me with judgment. They did not ask any questions surrounding the pregnancy. They tested me. The test was positive. They collected the money I received from the pastor. They sent me to the room for the procedure. Not once did they ask me if there was an adult with me or even if I had any questions about the procedure. Talk about cold. There was no emotional support given at all. I can remember being so afraid. I went to grab for the nurse's hand, but she quickly pulled her hand back and offered me a baby's diaper that was rolled up. How awful!!!! I was devastated. To add insult to injury, after the procedure, the pastor was there to pick me up. Then we drove close to my house. I got out of the car and walked the rest of the way home. The Pastor and the First Lady were joining us soon for dinner. I had to act as if I was not in pain, hold in my tears, and enjoy the evening.

A lack of supportive resources, understanding, or compassionate care during the abortion experience can contribute to feelings of guilt. If individuals perceive their decision as isolating or unsupported, it can intensify their emotional response. I battled for many months, following the procedure, with suicidal thoughts. I was depressed about the abortion. I had no one to talk to about it. I was too afraid to pray about it. So, I just held everything in. After the abortion, my life began to change for the better. I broke away from the pastor. I stopped going to their house. I ended the lessons with the First Lady. I had gotten a job. That was my way out without having to give a bunch of excuses for why I could not make it to lessons.

While working at one of the local grocery stores in my neighborhood, I became close friends with one of the other employees who had just recently relocated to the area. She shared some things with me, and she, too, had an abortion. I was too afraid to tell her my story, but she told me about a support group that she had gone through that really helped her. She was going through counseling there; she had been raped, and from that, she had gotten pregnant. This was the reason her family relocated to help her heal and start life again.

I wanted that so badly. I wanted to heal and have a fresh start in my life. I was just so afraid to start. I knew that I would have to talk about the things that had been done to me and the things that I had done. I daydreamed about what starting over would look like for me. I walked past that building for two years and I did not have the courage to go in there. Our community was so close-knit, and it seemed as if everybody knew you and your family. I wanted to spare my parents the hurt and the embarrassment. I did not want to bring shame on the pastor, either. The First Lady had gotten ill again and suddenly passed away. I was not ready to face that guilt either.

Seeking counseling or support groups can be beneficial in processing these emotions and finding ways to cope with guilt. Non-judgmental and compassionate discussions with trusted friends, family, or healthcare professionals can also help in navigating the feelings of guilt and finding healing and acceptance. Ultimately, individuals should prioritize their emotional well-being and seek the support they need to process their emotions and be able to move beyond their loss in a healthy way.

When I went off to college, that was when I began my healing journey. I was like my friend back home who got a new start. Relocating allowed me to face my truth. I began to write out my feelings, and this is what led me to pray. I was returning to God. I joined a small Christian support group that I learned about on campus. My counselor, as well as the group sessions that I attended, helped me to see that I was not alone and that God loved me.

My Act of Forgiveness

One day I openly shared what I had gone through. Our session opened with the story about the woman at the well. The weight of the guilt and shame just began to fall off. As I bitterly wept in repentance, I was being washed. I felt Jesus' love and His redemptive power embrace me. He was restoring me. I did not have to hide anymore. He already knew everything about me and yet He wanted to heal me through His love. This allowed me to come out and share my truth. Just as the woman at the well was able to receive her healing through her honesty, so did I.

It was difficult for me to even gather my thoughts when I thought of the pastor, not only because of what he did to me but also because of his soul. Oh my God. Every day he was at the church faithfully praying and preaching. "Lord, did he make it to heaven or is his soul rotting in hell" is a question that I quietly ask myself. Then, I quickly shake that question out of my mind.

I do hope that he and all of us make it right with our Heavenly Father through Jesus, and that we receive the gift of forgiveness as well as forgive others. We must come out of hiding and allow healing to manifest in our lives. We cannot afford to hide behind our titles, positions, or what we think others will say about us. Too many people are hurting. I stand firm on this.

There is trauma in the church and lives are at risk if we, the church and the body of Christ, refuse to address these issues. We, the people, must hold our government officials, policemen, teachers, community leaders, and clergymen accountable for their actions. We cannot be silent. We must be willing to have open communication that will foster healing for every one of us.

Jesus loves us so much that if we are willing to walk in our healing, then He will allow us to serve Him. The water that He pours into us so that we will never thirst again is the same water that will come from us as we serve Him (His people). I have gracefully accepted my calling and that is to extend that same grace of forgiveness that I received and help others do the same as they embrace their healing journey and forgive those who hurt them.

After she had received her healing, the Samaritan woman started sharing her story, even the ugly part of her story. This is why I am here today. I have dedicated my life to sharing where Jesus met me and how He restored me. I am victorious, and I want to help others (especially women and girls) who have experienced sexual abuse, unplanned pregnancy, and abortion know that they are victorious also.

Our past may have left scars, but we won't let them define us. We are survivors, and we have harnessed the extraordinary power of forgiveness to transform our lives. As we continue our journey we will support each other on this healing path with the knowledge that we are never alone. God called me to share what I had experienced—my imperfect life, the brokenness, the bitterness, the sex addiction, the abortion, and the hiding, so that people would understand that it is not about us being perfect in our own strength, but it is through Him that we are made perfect despite our shortcomings. Read the story John 4:1-29 and experience the healing journey that is waiting for you.

Reflection:

By forgiving others, I allow myself to fully engage in the wonderful aspects of my life. I choose to focus on the good parts of my life and to release the past. The past only has the power I choose to give it. I choose to be free of the past.

The New Beginning that Forgiveness Brings

In closing, forgiveness is a profound and transformative act that has the power to liberate us from the burdens of anger, resentment, and pain. Throughout this book, we have explored the complexities of forgiveness, the hurdles we face in the journey, and the tremendous rewards that await us on the other side.

Remember that forgiveness is not about condoning or excusing the wrongs done to us; it is about reclaiming our power and choosing compassion over bitterness. It is a gift we give ourselves, allowing us to heal, grow, and create space for new beginnings.

Forgiveness requires courage, vulnerability, and a willingness to confront our own pain. It is a process that takes time and self-compassion. Along the way, we may encounter setbacks, doubts, and moments of resistance, but know that you are not alone. Countless others have embarked on this journey before you, and their stories of resilience and transformation can inspire and guide you.

As you navigate the path of forgiveness, remember to be patient with yourself. Celebrate the small victories and milestones, for each step forward brings you closer to a place of inner peace and freedom. Embrace self-care, seek support from loved ones or professionals, and engage in practices that nourish your soul.

Forgiveness is a choice, and it is never too late to embark on this transformative journey. Whether you are forgiving others, yourself, or the circumstances of life, know that you have the capacity to release the past and embrace a future filled with hope, joy, and love.

May the lessons shared in this book serve as a guiding light, reminding you that forgiveness is a courageous act that can reshape your life. Embrace the power of forgiveness, and may it lead you to a life of profound healing, personal growth, and profound inner peace.

P.S. I would like to also thank those who shared their journey with us. You are truly Healing Ambassadors for the Kingdom.

With love and gratitude,

Coach Tonya

The Beauty of the Butterfly in You

In the cocoon's embrace, a transformation begins, a delicate journey where a new life begins. From the humble caterpillar, with its earthbound crawl, emerges a creature, breathtaking and tall.

From the depths of brokenness, emerging by grace, a symbol of Triumphant, taking its place. The journey of a butterfly, a lesson profound, that even in darkness, beauty can be found.

So let us remember, when life feels too small, that within us lies the power to rise, to stand tall. Like the butterfly, we too can transform, and embrace our true selves, in radiant form.

Embrace the process, the growth, and the pain, for it is in these moments, our strength we attain. Like the making of a butterfly, we too can rise, embracing our wings, with colors that mesmerize.

So let us spread our wings, with courage and might, and embark on a journey, radiant and bright. For within us, a butterfly lies in wait, ready to soar, and create our own fate.

Daily Affirmation

I forgive everyone in my past.

I am able to forgive everyone that has ever hurt me. I let go of negativity from previous experiences and set myself free from the prison of grudges, pain, and anger.

I remove the bitterness from my heart and mind. Holding onto this pain is unnecessary, unproductive, and keeps me a victim of my past. I choose to move forward into a life without it.

I eliminate the desire for revenge from my heart as I allow the universe and karma to handle things instead. I feel that it is important to let go and make peace. I reject past pain and anger. I get rid of the blame without residual sadness.

I notice the lightness I feel after letting go of the past and the people from it. I am able to find joy again because I forgive.

I forgive myself, too. I get rid of the constant reminders of previous mistakes and errors. I do what I can to make up for my mistakes, learn from them, and move on with a lighter heart.

Scripture Reflection on Forgiveness

Matthew 6:14
"For if you forgive other people when they sin against you, your heavenly Father will also forgive you."

Daniel 9:9
"The Lord our God is merciful and forgiving, even though we have rebelled against him."

Isaiah 43:25
"I, even I, am he who blots out your transgressions, for my own sake, and remembers your sins no more."

Ephesians 1:7-8
"In Him we have redemption through His blood, the forgiveness of sins, according to the riches of His grace which He made to abound toward us in all wisdom and prudence."

Colossians 1:13-14
"He has delivered us from the power of darkness and conveyed us into the kingdom of the Son of His love, in whom we have redemption through His blood, the forgiveness of sins."

Ephesians 4:31-32 NIV
31 Get rid of all bitterness, rage and anger, brawling and slander, along with every form of malice.

32 Be kind and compassionate to one another, forgiving each other, just as in Christ God forgave you.

Acts 3:19 NIV
19 Repent, then, and turn to God, so that your sins may be wiped out, that times of refreshing may come from the Lord.

About The Author

Tonya Maxwell enjoys living her life purposefully by God's grace as a wife, mother, daughter, sister, nana, and friend to many. As an author, CEO, and founder of Triumphators, LLC, she is passionate about helping her clients navigate through the event, experience, and the effect of their loss through storytelling, small group coaching workshops, and seminars. Her goal is to create a safe and empathetic space where women can explore the depths of human resilience, vulnerability, and personal growth as they embark upon their own healing journey.

Writing about trauma is a deeply personal and courageous endeavor for those who choose to share, whether you reveal it to one person or to many. As an author, Tonya Maxwell recognizes the importance of sharing stories that explore the complexities of human experiences, including those marked by trauma.

It is her belief that by shedding light on these narratives, we foster understanding, compassion, and the potential for healing. For over the past 35 years, she has recorded in her journals and many other forms of writing, her life-long healing journey: From Trauma to Triumph.

She believes that through the power of transparent storytelling, we can create meaningful dialogue, inspire change, and ultimately contribute to a more compassionate and supportive world in which we live.

Her motto is "Your story has beauty; your story has strength, and your story can help someone else. Write your new chapter and wear your crown."

References

The mental wellbeing of young people – with dr. Laura Hedayati. Baha'i Blog. (2022, November 20). https://www.bahaiblog.net/video/interview/bahai-blog-interviews-laura-hedayati/

Release the Butterflies Workbook

Forgiving Those Who Hurt You

The Power of Forgiveness Essential Key Elements

Even for the deepest of wounds, it is crucial to find a way to detach as much as possible from the pain. In most cases, this means to move into a state of forgiveness for the one who caused the wound.

1. Forgiveness is not about the other person. Forgiveness is strictly about me.

    - Your focus is to care for yourself. Forgiveness is completely about you. It is about your freedom, your peace, and your future.

2. Forgiving someone is **not** saying that person has no responsibility for what happened. Their actions caused pain and, yes, they are responsible for that pain.

3. Forgiving someone is not saying that I must stay in a relationship with them or be around them.

    - You do not have to be friends with or spend time with people who cause you to feel terrible about yourself. Forgiveness does not require this.

4. Forgiving someone does not make me weak.

5. Forgiveness is a choice that I can commit to.

Reflection:

1. What is your biggest concern about forgiving the person who hurt you the most?

2. Everyone has done something they are ashamed of. What is your biggest fear if you forgive yourself?

3. List all your reasons for not forgiving that person who hurt you so badly.

I acknowledge my feelings and forgive.

Today, I show forgiveness and move on from my past. I stop allowing the past to control me and my present. **I let go of it and the people who hurt me.** I get rid of the pain, sadness, anger, and resentment and replace them with new memories I can cherish.

Self-Reflection Questions:

How can I forgive people without letting them hurt me again?

____

____

____

Where can I get more help to learn forgiveness?

____

____

____

What can I do to make it easier for me to forgive and move on?

____

____

____

Forgiveness = Freedom

Now that you know that forgiveness isn't about spending time with toxic people or giving away your power, it's time to look at what forgiveness is.

Very simply, forgiveness is FREEDOM.

- Freedom from having what happened always on your mind
- Freedom from the anger and fear
- Freedom from having to grit your teeth when you see them

As difficult as forgiveness can be, it lightens the load on your mind, brings peace to your heart, and frees you to move forward to the future.

Refusing Forgiveness Affects All Areas of Your Life

Holding onto pain and resentment has major negative effects on you. You'll find you're easily distracted by the pain, and this limits your ability to be fully productive. You also miss the joys of life.

When you relive what happened, your body reacts as if you just experienced the pain. You feel like a victim and have difficulty accessing your inner strength.

Holding onto emotional pain weakens you. You are like the powerful elephant prevented from moving because it believes the little chain around its ankle controls its life.

Let's examine more deeply what forgiveness gives you:

1. **Forgiveness gives you the power to move into the future.** When you are hurt, no matter how badly, you can feel like you are carrying around a ball and chain. You hold it so tightly that you have forgotten how to release it. If you allow it, that wound can lock you into pain and keep you from seeing the beauty in life.

    - **When you release the pain, you unchain yourself and throw away the chain and everything attached to it.**

    - Your body responds with an "Ahhh" and releases energy. This allows you to make plans for the future and open your heart to reviving neglected relationships and meeting new people.

2. **No longer are you defined by your wound.** Forgiveness allows you to be the amazing, wonderful person you are. Before you release the pain from that terrible hurt, you're defined as the one whose partner betrayed you, or whose boss falsely accused and fired you.

    - Avoid being defined by what happened to you. Define yourself by overcoming what happened and being more successful and happier than anyone thought you could be.

    - **When you do not focus on the past, you will find your path to happiness, the gifts and talents you've forgotten, and the strength to look fear in the eye and go through it.**

- The pain will have changed you, but when you release it, *you* choose to determine what happens to you, not someone else.

3. **When you forgive, the other person no longer has control of you.**

    - When you do not forgive, the person who hurt you has control of you. They are on your mind, occupying your thoughts, sapping your energy, perhaps determining where you go, who you see, and what you do… and they do not have to say a word.

    - Enough of that. Choose to not let them control your thoughts and emotions. Letting it all go demonstrates that they cannot control you. You control what you hold onto and what you release.

4. **You get to make the powerful choice of releasing the pain and moving into freedom.**

    - You will no longer be caught in victim consciousness. Victim consciousness has you believing you are powerless, making it difficult for you to take positive steps for the future.

    - You demonstrate what a powerful person you are to let something go that many people cannot. **It takes great personal power to forgive.**

    - No longer will you be hypervigilant, fearing similar injuries in relationships. **Your true self will shine through improving current and future relationships.**

5. **Your physical health improves.** When you forgive, there are powerful changes in the body which lead to a healthier and longer life.

    - In the last few decades, biologists and medical researchers have discovered the power of the mind-body connection. They have found that holding onto emotional pain affects the body mentally, emotionally, and physically.

6. **Health benefits of forgiveness**

    - Lower blood pressure
    - Stronger immune system
    - Better heart health
    - Less stress, which improves digestion, sexual response, sleep, and more
    - Lower risk of anxiety and depression
    - Improved relationships, which are known to strengthen your immune system, increase the "feel good" chemicals in your body, and reduce stress

As you can see, forgiving someone is one of the most powerful choices you can make to improve your life physically, mentally, emotionally, and spiritually. This makes positive changes in your relationships.

Summary

Now that you know the positive effects forgiveness can have in every area of your life, the question you may be asking is, "How do I forgive?" In the next module, you will explore various methods which have proven to assist in forgiveness. **The key is finding the one that works for you.**

Reflection

1. Think of someone who has hurt you and you haven't forgiven. Notice what happens to your body and how your thoughts and emotions change. Now write about what you noticed.

2. Bring to mind someone you love and feel comfortable with. Notice the changes in your body, mind, and emotions. List what you have noticed.

3. What do you want to achieve by forgiving someone?

Understanding Forgiveness

The number of hurts and types of hurt you have suffered in the past, combined with your thoughts and beliefs, can make it difficult to release the past. When you add the biochemical response of your body, it is a wonder anyone can forgive another.

In this module, you will learn that your view of forgiveness can add to the difficulty of putting the past behind you. In this short module, you will explore what forgiveness is and what forgiveness is not. This knowledge will assist you in letting go of the hurt and moving forward in life with joy.

Forgiveness benefits all areas of your life. Your emotional and physical health will improve. You will be able to think more clearly and move into the future with confidence and joy.

Now, all you need to know is how to accomplish this healing and life-giving process. That is what you will learn in the next module.

To prepare for what comes next, please take a few minutes right now to reflect on the following. This will prepare your subconscious mind for your next step into personal power.

Reflection:

Allow yourself to answer the following as fully as you can. Write what comes to you. Allow your mind to flow.

1. When I am no longer saddled with the pain of *it,* I will be able to:

2. Write out why a future without emotional pain is better than feeling the way you do now.

Forgiveness restores my peace of mind.

When I forgive others, I also liberate myself from being weighed down by past events. I wipe the slate clean and start anew.

Forgiveness puts me back in control of my life. I focus on my own reactions rather than external events. My resilience increases as I become more skillful at dealing with conflicts and disappointments.

Letting go of resentment reduces my anxiety. I know from experience that I commit many actions for which I need to be pardoned. ***It is important to teach myself that absolution is possible.***

Most of all, I take pleasure in knowing that I promote healing when I make allowances for mistakes and misjudgments.

A tolerant attitude helps me to better understand someone who hurts me. They may be feeling pressured or experiencing great losses.

When I respond with kindness rather than anger, we all have the opportunity to grow.

Absolution becomes easier and more constructive when I accept accountability for my role in any clashes. I am honest with myself about my shortcomings.

Distinguishing between people and their actions helps me to protect my own welfare while turning the other cheek. ***I understand I can feel affection and concern for others without condoning behavior that contradicts my values.***

Forgiveness becomes more automatic as I rejoice in the good feelings it brings.

Today, I throw away grudges from the past. I enjoy the peace of mind that comes with extending forgiveness.

Self-Reflection Questions:

1. What are the barriers that make it difficult for me to forgive?

2. How does forgiveness make me happier?

3. Is there one person I could choose to forgive today?

Forgiveness is a gift I give to myself.

While I may have been wronged in the past, I choose to forgive others. Forgiveness is a gift I give myself. By forgiving others, I become free of the past. I am then free to live entirely in the present.

Forgiveness sometimes seems like a gift I am giving to others, but it is really something I do for myself. Holding onto the past creates challenges in the present and future, so I choose to let go of the past and move forward without baggage.

I am grateful for the challenges of my past. These challenges teach valuable lessons that I can use in the present.

By forgiving others, I allow myself to fully engage in the wonderful aspects of my life. I choose to focus on the good parts of my life and to release the past. The past only has the power I choose to give it. I choose to be free of the past.

When I feel that I have been treated poorly, I search for the valuable lesson in that situation. Then I forgive and forget. I am mistreating myself when I hold onto a grudge.

Forgiveness is a way of showing strength and compassion to others and myself.

Today, I give myself a gift by forgiving others for their transgressions against me. I feel light and free as a bird when I practice forgiveness.

Self-Reflection Questions:

1. Whom do I need to forgive?

2. What would I gain by forgiving that person?

3. Can I let go of my negative feelings about that person?

Notes

Notes

Notes

Notes

Notes

Notes

Notes

Notes

Notes

Notes

To connect with Tonya Maxwell and Live Triumphantly,

visit Triumphantors, LLC

https://www.facebook.com/livingtriumphantly247/

https://www.instagram.com/maxwell.tonya/

https://www.tiktok.com/@tonyamaxwell04

https://www.youtube.com/tonyamaxwelltriumphato
rsspeaks

Or call 1-888-248-2874

Made in United States
Troutdale, OR
11/04/2025

41246878R00058